CHRISTMAS IN
THE BUSHVELD

By: K.A. Mulenga

© Kalenga Augustine Mulenga

CHRISTMAS IN THE BUSHVELD

Published by Kalenga Augustine Mulenga

Johannesburg, South Africa

augustine@kamulenga.com

ISBN 978-0-6398-9549-9

2 4 6 8 10 9 7 5 3 1

Illustration and layout by Boutique Books

I dedicate this book to my wife Sheba and my kids, Grace, Malaika and Kalenga Jr.

Thank you for believing in me!

In a small village nestled in the African bushveld, a young girl named Lerato sat outside her home, gazing at the sky. It was Christmas Eve and, as the sun set in a blaze of orange and gold, she couldn't stop thinking about one thing: snow. She had seen pictures of snow-covered trees and frosty rooftops in books, and she wished that, just once, she could experience a white Christmas.

Her grandfather, Umkhulu Thabo, noticed her sitting quietly. He walked over and sat beside her, his walking stick making a soft thud on the dry earth. "What's on your mind, Lerato?" he asked gently.

"I'm dreaming of a white Christmas, Umkhulu," she replied. "Like the ones in the stories. With snow and ice and big, sparkling trees."

Umkhulu Thabo chuckled softly. "Ah, my child," he said, "snow is beautiful, but so is the Christmas we have here in the bushveld. Come, let me show you the magic of our Christmas traditions."

Lerato followed her grandfather as he led her to the centre of the village, where a large baobab tree stood proudly. The villagers had gathered, ready to decorate the tree for their Christmas celebration. Instead of glittery ornaments, they used handmade decorations crafted from beads, woven grass and colourful fabrics.

"Look," Umkhulu Thabo said, handing Lerato a string of bright beads. "Each of these beads represents something special. Love, family, friendship. This tree will remind us of the things we hold dear."

Lerato smiled as she carefully hung the beads on the tree. Other children added clay animals, small wooden carvings and ribbons in the colours of the earth – deep reds, greens and golds. Soon, the baobab tree sparkled under the warm evening sky.

Next, Umkhulu Thabo led Lerato back to their home, where her mother and aunts were busy preparing a Christmas feast. The air was filled with the delicious smell of roasted chicken, grilled vegetables and freshly baked bread.

"Food brings people together," Umkhulu said. "In our village, we share everything with our friends and neighbours. This is how we celebrate Christmas – by giving to one another."

Lerato helped her mother stir the big pot of stew and watched as the women placed bowls of food in the centre of the village square.

As the stars began to twinkle above, the whole village gathered to enjoy the feast together. There was laughter, singing, and the joyful sounds of drums and flutes.

Lerato's heart felt warm as she saw everyone sharing food, stories and love. She realised that, while she had once dreamed of snow, this Christmas was perfect in its own way.

"See, my child?" Umkhulu Thabo said, his eyes twinkling. "Our Christmas may not have snow, but it is filled with the warmth of our traditions, family and the beauty of our land."

Lerato hugged her grandfather tightly. "You're right, Umkhulu," she said. "This is the most beautiful Christmas I could ever imagine."

And so, under the starry African sky, Lerato celebrated Christmas in the bushveld, surrounded by her family, friends and the magic of their rich, vibrant traditions.

THE END

By K.A. Mulenga

Chuck the Cheetah
Cam, the Courageous Camaro
Christmas in the Bushveld
David, the great king
Donk and the Stubborn Donkeys
Drew, the Dragon
Elaine the Elephant
Four seasons in one day
Harry the Honest Horse
Imbwa, the Story Of the Dog and His Harsh Master
Jesus, the Baby King
Joe Finds His Way Home
Max the Gorilla
Malaika and the Magic Christmas Tree
Monty the Monkey and the Missing Rhinos
Never Give Up
Never Give Up 2 - The Miracle Game
Never Give Up 3 - Even Goalkeepers can Score
Never Give Up 4 - The Topsy Turvy Cup Match
Never Give Up 5 - The Comeback Match
Never Give Up 6 - It Was Meant To Be
Never Give Up 7 - The Amazing Adventure
Patty the Pink Pug
Piggly the Angry Piglet
Polly the Polecat
Robbie the Raven and Debbie the Dove
Rudy, the Reindeer Who Could Not Fly
Spike and Spud , the Spaceboys
Susie Strickland, Sizzling Striker
Susie Strickland, Sizzling Striker 2 - The New School
The Christmas Cookie Contest
The Leopard Licks Its Spots
The Lion and the Impala
The Weaver Birds
Tumelo's Safari Christmas Adventure
Will and His Best Friend Whale

Thank you for reading Christmas in the Bushveld. I hope
you enjoyed it! Please let K.A. Mulenga know about what you
thought about the book by leaving a short review on Amazon, it
will help other parents and children find the story.
(If you're under 13, ask a grown up to help you)

Top Tip: Be sure not to give away any of the story's secrets!

Sign up to my readers' club weekly newsletter.
Simply click on the YES, SIGN ME UP button on my website.
I will never share your email address. Unsubscribe at any time.

www.ingramcontent.com/pod-product-compliance
Lightning Source LLC
Chambersburg PA
CBHW041559040426
42447CB00002B/226